SOFTWARE DEVELOPMENT MANAGER GUIDE

People | Process | Tools | Delivery

Adrian Krzesniak

Contents

1. Introduction

1.1. Purpose of the book

In the rapidly evolving world of software development, the role of a software development manager is both challenging and rewarding. This book aims to serve as a comprehensive guide for current and aspiring software development managers, providing insights and practical advice on how to effectively lead teams, manage processes, utilize tools, and ensure successful delivery of projects.

The primary purpose of this book is to:

➢ Empower managers: Equip managers with the knowledge and skills needed to navigate the complexities of software development. From building and motivating teams to optimizing processes and leveraging the right tools, this book covers all essential aspects of management.

➢ Enhance understanding: Offer a deep understanding of the software development lifecycle and various methodologies such as Agile and Scrum. By understanding these processes, managers can better plan, execute, and deliver projects.

➢ Provide practical tools: Introduce essential tools and techniques that can streamline project management, improve collaboration, and enhance productivity. This includes project management software, version control systems, and CI/CD pipelines.

- Focus on delivery: Highlight strategies for effective planning, risk management, and delivering value to stakeholders. Ensuring timely and quality delivery is crucial for the success of any software project.

- By the end of this book, readers will have a solid foundation in software development management, equipped with the tools and strategies needed to lead their teams to success. Whether you are new to management or looking to refine your skills, this book is designed to be a valuable resource on your journey.

1.2. Who should read this book

This book is designed for a diverse audience, ranging from seasoned professionals to those just starting their journey in software development management. Whether you are an experienced manager looking to refine your skills or a developer aspiring to move into a leadership role, this book offers valuable insights and practical guidance.

- Current software development managers: If you are already in a management position, this book will help you enhance your leadership skills, optimize processes, and stay updated with the latest tools and methodologies. It provides strategies to tackle common challenges and improve team performance.

- Aspiring managers: For developers and technical leads who aspire to transition into management roles, this book serves as a comprehensive guide. It covers the essential aspects of management, from building and leading teams to managing projects and delivering successful outcomes.

➢ Project managers and team leads: Those who are responsible for overseeing software development projects will find this book particularly useful. It offers practical advice on project planning, risk management, and ensuring timely delivery, helping you to effectively manage your projects and teams.

➢ HR professionals and recruiters: Understanding the dynamics of software development teams and the skills required for effective management can be beneficial for HR professionals and recruiters. This book provides insights into team building, talent retention, and conflict resolution, which are crucial for creating a productive work environment.

➢ Students and educators: Students pursuing degrees in computer science, software engineering, or related fields, as well as educators teaching these subjects, can benefit from this book. It offers a real-world perspective on software development management, bridging the gap between academic knowledge and industry practices.

➢ Anyone interested in software development: Even if you are not directly involved in software development but have an interest in understanding how software projects are managed and delivered, this book provides a comprehensive overview. It demystifies the complexities of software development management and offers insights into the industry.

By catering to a wide range of readers, this book aims to be a valuable resource for anyone interested in the field of software development management. Whether you are looking to enhance your current skills or gain new knowledge, this book is designed to support your professional growth and success.

1.3. Overview of software development management

Software development management is a multifaceted discipline that involves overseeing the development, maintenance, and delivery of software products. It requires a blend of technical knowledge, leadership skills, and strategic thinking to ensure that projects are completed successfully and meet the needs of stakeholders. This section provides an overview of the key components and responsibilities involved in software development management.

➢ Role of a software development manager:
- The software development manager is responsible for leading a team of developers, coordinating project activities, and ensuring that software products are delivered on time and within budget. This role involves setting goals, managing resources, and fostering a collaborative work environment.

➢ Key Responsibilities:
- Team leadership: Building and leading a high-performing development team. This includes recruiting talent (together with Talent Acquisition), providing mentorship, and creating a positive work culture.
- Project management: Planning, executing, and monitoring software development projects (often with project managers or PMO Project Management

Office as well as product management). This involves defining project scope, setting milestones, and managing timelines.

- Process optimization: Implementing and refining development processes to improve efficiency and quality. This includes adopting methodologies like Agile and Scrum and continuously seeking ways to optimize workflows.
- Stakeholder communication: Engaging with stakeholders to understand their requirements and expectations. Stakeholders can be understood as customers or product management representatives (product owners in Scrum or product managers). Effective communication ensures that the development team is aligned with business goals and delivers value to stakeholders.
- Risk management: Identifying and mitigating risks that could impact project success. This involves proactive planning and problem-solving to address potential challenges.
- Overseeing Software Development Life Cycle (SDLC): Understanding the SDLC is crucial for effective management. The SDLC includes stages such as planning, analysis, design, implementation, testing, deployment, and maintenance. Each stage requires careful coordination and management to ensure smooth progression and successful delivery.

➢ Development methodologies: Various methodologies can be employed to manage software development projects. Agile, Scrum, and SAFe are popular choices due to their flexibility and iterative approach. These methodologies emphasize collaboration, continuous improvement, and adaptability to changing requirements.

➢ Tools and technologies: Effective software development management involves leveraging the right tools and technologies. Project management software, version control systems, and CI/CD pipelines are essential for streamlining workflows, enhancing collaboration, and ensuring quality.

➢ Quality assurance: Ensuring the quality of software products is a critical aspect of management. This involves implementing testing strategies, conducting code reviews, and maintaining high standards of quality throughout the development process.

➢ Delivery and deployment: Successful delivery involves careful planning, managing deadlines, and ensuring that the final product meets stakeholder expectations. Deployment strategies must be well-coordinated to minimize disruptions and ensure smooth transitions.

➢ Continuous improvement: Software development management is an ongoing process of learning and improvement. Managers must stay updated with industry trends, adopt the best practices, and continuously seek ways to enhance team performance and project outcomes.

By understanding these key components, software development managers can effectively lead their teams, manage projects, and deliver high-quality software products. This overview sets the foundation for the detailed exploration of people, processes, tools, and delivery in the subsequent sections of this book.

2. People

2.1. Building and leading a development team

Building and leading a development team is one of the most critical responsibilities of a software development manager. A well-constructed team can significantly impact the success of projects and the overall productivity of the organization. This chapter explores the key aspects of assembling and guiding a high-performing development team.

Identifying team needs

The first step in building a development team is understanding the specific needs of your projects and organization. This involves:

➢ Defining roles and responsibilities: Clearly outline the roles required for your team (together with Human Resources), such as developers, testers, designers, DevOps, scrum masters, product owners, and project managers. Each role should have defined responsibilities and expectations.
➢ Assessing skills and competencies: Identify the technical and soft skills needed for each role. This includes programming languages, frameworks, problem-solving abilities, and communication skills.

Recruiting and hiring

Effective recruitment is essential for building a strong team. Consider the following strategies:

➢ Creating detailed job descriptions: Write clear and comprehensive job descriptions that accurately reflect roles and responsibilities. Highlight the skills and experience required.
➢ Utilizing multiple recruitment channels (in cooperation with Talent Acquisition). Use various channels to reach potential candidates, including job boards, social media, employee referrals, professional networks, and recruitment agencies.

> Conducting thorough interviews: Develop a structured interview process that assesses both technical skills and cultural fit. Include coding tests, problem-solving exercises, and behavioral interviews.

Onboarding and integration

A smooth onboarding process helps new team members integrate quickly and effectively:

> Providing comprehensive orientation: Introduce new hires to the company culture, values, and processes. Provide an overview of ongoing projects and the tools used by the team.

> Assigning mentors or buddies: Pair new team members with experienced mentors who can guide them through their initial period. Mentors can help with technical challenges and provide support in adapting to the team dynamics.

> Setting clear expectations: Communicate the goals, expectations, and performance metrics from the outset. Ensure new hires understand their roles and how their contributions align with the team's objectives.

Fostering a collaborative environment

Creating a collaborative and inclusive environment is crucial for team success:

> Encouraging open communication: Promote a culture of transparency and open communication. Encourage team members to share ideas, provide feedback, and voice concerns.

> Building trust and respect: Foster mutual trust and respect among team members. Recognize and appreciate individual contributions and celebrate team achievements.

> Facilitating team-building activities: Organize regular team-building activities to strengthen relationships and

improve collaboration. These can include workshops, social events, and team outings.

Providing continuous support and development

Supporting your team's growth and development is key to maintaining high performance:

➢ Offering training and development opportunities: Provide access to training programs, workshops, and conferences. Encourage continuous learning and skill development.
➢ Conducting regular performance reviews: Schedule regular performance reviews to discuss progress, provide constructive feedback, and set new goals. Use these reviews to identify areas for improvement and recognize achievements.
➢ Promoting career growth: Support career advancement by offering opportunities for promotion, role changes, and increased responsibilities. Help team members set and achieve their career goals.

Managing conflicts and challenges

Effective conflict management is essential for maintaining a positive team environment:

➢ Addressing issues promptly: Tackle conflicts and issues as soon as they arise. Use a fair and impartial approach to resolve disputes and find mutually acceptable solutions.
➢ Encouraging constructive feedback: Create a culture where constructive feedback is valued and encouraged. Teach team members how to give and receive feedback in a positive and productive manner.

Leading by example

As a manager, your behavior sets the tone for the team:

11

➢ Demonstrating integrity and accountability: Lead with integrity and take responsibility for your actions. Show that you are accountable and expect the same from your team.

➢ Being approachable and supportive: Be accessible and approachable to your team members. Offer support and guidance when needed and create an environment where team members feel comfortable seeking help.

➢ Inspiring and motivating: Inspire your team by setting a positive example and demonstrating passion for your work. Motivate your team by recognizing their efforts and celebrating successes.

By focusing on these key aspects, you can build and lead a development team that is motivated, collaborative, and capable of delivering high-quality software products. The success of your team depends on your ability to create a supportive environment, provide continuous development opportunities, and lead with integrity and vision.

2.2. Effective communication & collaboration

Effective communication and collaboration

Effective communication and collaboration are the cornerstones of a successful software development team. They ensure that team members are aligned, informed, and working together towards common goals. This section explores strategies and best practices for fostering strong communication and collaboration within your team.

Importance of communication

Clear and consistent communication is essential for:

- ➢ Aligning goals and expectations: Ensuring that everyone understands the project objectives, their roles, and the expected outcomes.
- ➢ Facilitating problem-solving: Encouraging open discussions to identify and resolve issues quickly.
- ➢ Building trust and transparency: Creating an environment where team members feel comfortable sharing ideas and feedback.

Communication channels

Utilize various communication channels to meet different needs:

- ➢ Face-to-Face meetings: Regular team meetings, one-on-one sessions, and stand-ups are crucial for direct and immediate communication. If the meeting is virtual, conduct it with the camera switched on.
- ➢ Digital communication tools: Use tools like Slack, Microsoft Teams, or email for quick updates, asynchronous communication, and documentation.
- ➢ Project management software: Platforms like Jira, Trello, or Asana help track progress, assign tasks, and keep everyone informed about project status.

Best practices for effective communication

Implement these best practices to enhance communication within your team:

- ➢ Active listening: Encourage team members to listen actively and attentively to each other. This fosters mutual understanding and respect.
- ➢ Clear and concise messaging: Communicate clearly and concisely to avoid misunderstandings. Use simple language and be specific about your expectations.
- ➢ Regular updates: Provide regular updates on project progress, changes, and any issues that arise. This keeps everyone informed and aligned.

> Feedback culture: Promote a culture of constructive feedback. Encourage team members to give and receive feedback positively and use it for continuous improvement.

Collaboration techniques

Effective collaboration involves working together efficiently and harmoniously:

> Agile practices: Implement Agile practices like daily stand-ups, sprint planning, and retrospectives to enhance collaboration and adaptability.
> Cross-functional teams: Build cross-functional teams with diverse skills and perspectives. This enhances problem-solving and innovation.
> Collaborative tools: Use collaborative tools like GitHub, Confluence, or Google Workspace to facilitate real-time collaboration and document sharing.

Building a collaborative culture

Create a culture that values and promotes collaboration:

> Shared vision and goals: Ensure that the team has a shared vision and common goals. This aligns their efforts and fosters a sense of purpose.
> Inclusive environment: Create an inclusive environment where all team members feel valued and respected. Encourage diverse perspectives and ideas. The best idea should always win.
> Team-building activities: Organize team-building activities to strengthen relationships and improve collaboration. These can include workshops, hackathons, and social events.
> Recognition and rewards: Recognize and reward collaborative efforts. Celebrate team achievements and individual contributions to foster a collaborative spirit.

Overcoming communication barriers

Address common communication barriers to ensure smooth collaboration:

➢ Language and cultural differences: Be mindful of language and cultural differences within the team. Provide language support if needed and promote cultural awareness.
➢ Remote work challenges: Address challenges related to remote work, such as time zone differences and lack of face-to-face interaction. Use video conferencing and collaboration tools to bridge the gap.
➢ Conflict resolution: Implement conflict resolution strategies to address and resolve conflicts promptly. Encourage open dialogue and find mutually acceptable solutions.

By focusing on effective communication and collaboration, you can create a cohesive and high-performing development team. These practices not only improve productivity but also enhance team morale and job satisfaction, leading to better project outcomes and a positive work environment.

2.3. Motivating and retaining talent

Motivating and retaining talent is crucial for maintaining a high-performing development team. A motivated team is more productive, innovative, and committed to achieving project goals. This section explores strategies for keeping your team engaged and ensuring long-term retention.

Understanding motivation

To effectively motivate your team, it's important to understand what drives them:

➢ Intrinsic motivation: this involves internal factors such as personal growth, job satisfaction, and a sense of accomplishment. Encouraging autonomy, mastery, and purpose can enhance intrinsic motivation.
➢ Extrinsic motivation: external factors like salary, bonuses, and recognition play a role in motivating team members. Providing competitive compensation and rewards can boost extrinsic motivation.

Creating a positive work environment

A positive work environment is essential for motivation:

➢ Fostering a supportive culture: Create a culture where team members feel supported and valued. Encourage collaboration, open communication, and mutual respect.
➢ Providing a comfortable workspace: Ensure that the physical workspace is comfortable and conducive to productivity. This includes ergonomic furniture, adequate lighting, and necessary equipment.
➢ Promoting work-life balance: Encourage a healthy work-life balance by offering flexible working hours, remote work options, and promoting time off. This helps prevent burnout and maintains motivation. Depending on company constraints, look for the best approaches within company rule boundaries.

Recognizing and rewarding achievements

Recognition and rewards are powerful motivators:

➢ Acknowledging contributions: Regularly acknowledge and appreciate individual and team contributions. This can be done through verbal praise, written notes, or public recognition.

- Offering incentives: Provide incentives such as bonuses, promotions, and awards for outstanding performance. Tailor rewards to individual preferences to make them more meaningful.
- Celebrating milestones: Celebrate project milestones and team achievements. Organize events or activities to mark these occasions and show appreciation for the team's hard work.

Providing growth and development opportunities

Continuous growth and development are key to retaining talent:

- Training and development programs: Offer access to training programs, workshops, and conferences. Encourage team members to pursue certifications and further education.
- Career advancement: Support career advancement by providing opportunities for promotion, role changes, and increased responsibilities. Help team members set and achieve their career goals.
- Mentorship and coaching: Implement mentorship and coaching programs to provide guidance and support. Pair team members with experienced mentors who can help them grow professionally.

Encouraging autonomy and empowerment

Empowering your team can boost motivation and engagement:

- Delegating responsibility: Delegate tasks and responsibilities to team members, allowing them to take ownership of their work. This fosters a sense of autonomy and accountability.
- Encouraging innovation: Create an environment where team members feel encouraged to innovate and

experiment. Support their ideas and provide the resources needed to explore new solutions.

> Involving team in decision-making: Involve the team in decision-making processes. Seek their input and feedback on project plans, strategies, and changes. This makes them feel valued and invested in the project's success.

Building Strong Relationships

Strong relationships within the team contribute to motivation and retention:

> Team-building activities: Organize team-building activities to strengthen relationships and improve collaboration. These can include workshops, social events, and team outings.
> Regular check-ins: Conduct regular one-on-one check-ins with team members to discuss their progress, challenges, and career aspirations. Show genuine interest in their well-being and development.
> Creating a sense of community: Foster a sense of community within the team. Encourage social interactions, support networks, and a collaborative spirit.

By implementing these strategies, you can create a motivated and engaged development team that is committed to achieving project goals and staying with the organization long-term. Motivating and retaining talent is an ongoing process that requires attention, support, and a genuine commitment to the well-being and growth of your team.

2.4. Managing conflicts and challenges

Managing conflicts and challenges

Conflicts and challenges are inevitable in any team environment, especially in the fast-paced world of software development. Effective management of these issues is crucial for maintaining a positive and productive work environment. This section explores strategies for identifying, addressing, and resolving conflicts and challenges within your team.

Identifying conflicts and challenges

The first step in managing conflicts and challenges is recognizing them early:

> ➢ Observing team dynamics: Pay attention to changes in team dynamics, such as increased tension, reduced communication, or changes in behavior. These can be indicators of underlying conflicts.
> ➢ Encouraging open communication: Create an environment where team members feel comfortable discussing their concerns and challenges. Encourage them to speak up about issues before they escalate.
> ➢ Regular check-ins: conduct regular one-on-one and team meetings to check in on progress, address concerns, and identify potential conflicts early.

Addressing conflicts

When conflicts arise, it's important to address them promptly and effectively:

> ➢ Active listening: Listen to all parties involved in the conflict without interrupting. Show empathy and understanding and acknowledge their perspectives.
> ➢ Neutral mediation: Act as a neutral mediator to facilitate a constructive dialogue between conflicting parties. Help them express their concerns and work towards a mutually acceptable solution.
> ➢ Finding common ground: Identify common goals and interests that both parties share. Use these as a

19

foundation to build a resolution that satisfies everyone involved.

> Setting clear expectations: Clearly communicate the expected behavior and outcomes. Ensure that all parties understand the resolution and their roles in maintaining it.

Implementing conflict resolution strategies

Use proven conflict resolution strategies to manage and resolve conflicts:

> Collaborative problem-solving: Encourage a collaborative approach to problem-solving. Involve all parties in brainstorming solutions and making decisions.
> Compromise and negotiation: Facilitate compromise and negotiation to find a middle ground that addresses the needs and concerns of all parties.
> Mediation and facilitation: Use mediation and facilitation techniques to guide discussions and help conflicting parties reach a resolution.
> Escalation procedures: Establish clear escalation procedures for conflicts that cannot be resolved at the team level. Involve higher management or HR if necessary.

Managing challenges

Challenges can arise from various sources, including technical issues, resource constraints, and external factors:

> Proactive planning: Anticipate potential challenges and plan accordingly. Develop contingency plans and allocate resources to address unexpected issues.
> Risk management: Implement risk management strategies to identify, assess, and mitigate risks. Regularly review and update risk management plans.
> Resource allocation: Ensure that your team has the necessary resources, including tools, training, and

support, to overcome challenges. Address any resource gaps promptly.

➢ Continuous improvement: Foster a culture of continuous improvement. Encourage team members to learn from challenges and implement changes to prevent similar issues in the future.

Learning from conflicts and challenges

Use conflicts and challenges as opportunities for growth and improvement:

➢ Reflecting on experiences: Reflect on conflicts and challenges to understand their root causes and identify lessons learned. Use these insights to improve team dynamics and processes.

➢ Implementing changes: Implement changes based on the lessons learned. This can include process improvements, new communication strategies, or updated conflict resolution procedures.

➢ Sharing knowledge: Share knowledge and experiences with the team. Encourage open discussions about conflicts and challenges to promote a culture of learning and continuous improvement.

By effectively managing conflicts and challenges, you can maintain a positive and productive work environment. These strategies not only help resolve issues but also strengthen team cohesion, improve communication, and enhance overall performance.

3. Process

3.1. Understanding Agile SDLC

Agile methodology revolutionizes the traditional Software Development Life Cycle (SDLC) by emphasizing flexibility, collaboration, and iterative progress. Agile breaks down the development process into smaller, manageable increments called sprints, allowing teams to adapt to changes and deliver value continuously. This chapter explores the Agile approach to SDLC and its key stages.

Planning and initiation

In Agile, planning is iterative and ongoing. Key activities include:

➢ Product vision and roadmap: Define the overall vision and roadmap for the product. This provides a high-level direction and goals.
➢ Backlog creation: Develop a product backlog that lists all requirements, features, enhancements. Prioritize items based on business value and stakeholder input.
➢ Sprint planning: Plan each sprint by selecting backlog items to be completed. Set clear objectives and define the scope for the sprint.

Requirements and user stories

Agile focuses on user stories to capture requirements:

➢ User stories: Write user stories that describe features from the end-user's perspective. Each story should include acceptance criteria to define when it is considered complete.
➢ Backlog refinement: Continuously refine and prioritize the backlog. Collaborate with stakeholders to ensure that user stories are clear, complete, and aligned with business goals.

Sometimes customers still use classic requirements to define their needs. Therefore, consider the connection between features or user stories and classic requirements to keep the requirements matrix clear.

Design and prototyping

Design in Agile is iterative and collaborative:

➤ Collaborative design: Involve the team in design discussions and brainstorming sessions. Use techniques like whiteboarding and wireframing to visualize ideas.
➤ Prototyping: Develop prototypes to validate design concepts and gather feedback. Iterate on designs based on feedback and testing results.

Development and coding

Development in Agile is incremental and iterative:

➤ Sprint execution: During each sprint, the team works on coding and implementing user stories. Follow coding standards and best practices.
➤ Continuous integration: Integrate code frequently to detect issues early. Use automated tests to ensure that new code does not break existing functionality.
➤ Pair Programming: Encourage pair programming to improve code quality and foster collaboration. The concept of pair programming can be adapted to develop together with an AI tool as the second developer.

Testing and quality assurance

Testing is integrated throughout the Agile process:

➤ Automated testing: Implement automated tests to verify functionality continuously. This includes unit tests, integration tests, and end-to-end tests. Try to use AI tools to generate non-productive code to speed up product development.

- ➢ Continuous feedback: Gather feedback from stakeholders and users regularly. Use this feedback to refine and improve the product.
- ➢ Sprint reviews: Conduct sprint reviews to demonstrate completed work and gather feedback. This helps ensure that the product meets user expectations.

Deployment and release

Deployment in Agile is frequent and incremental:

- ➢ Continuous deployment: Deploy changes frequently to production. Use automated deployment pipelines to streamline the process.
- ➢ Release planning: Plan releases based on business needs and stakeholder priorities. Ensure that each release delivers valuable features and improvements.
- ➢ User training and support: Provide training and support to users for new features. Create documentation and conduct training sessions as needed.

Maintenance and continuous improvement

Maintenance in Agile is ongoing and iterative:

- ➢ Bug fixes: Address issues and bugs promptly. In every sprint, allocate a percentage of capacity for these tasks in every sprint.
- ➢ Product updates: Release patches and updates regularly to improve the product.
- ➢ Cybersecurity: Address vulnerabilities and update libraries promptly. Allocate a percentage of capacity for these tasks in every sprint.
- ➢ Enhancements: Continuously enhance the product based on user feedback, product management feedback, and changing requirements. Prioritize enhancements in the backlog.
- ➢ Retrospectives: Conduct regular retrospectives to reflect on the team's performance and identify areas for

improvement. Implement changes to enhance processes and collaboration.

Importance of Agile SDLC

Agile SDLC offers several benefits:

➤ Flexibility and adaptability: Agile allows teams to adapt to changes and evolving requirements. This ensures that the product remains relevant and valuable.
➤ Continuous delivery: Agile promotes continuous delivery of value through frequent releases. This helps stakeholders see progress and benefit from new features regularly.
➤ Collaboration and transparency: Agile fosters collaboration and transparency among team members and stakeholders. This improves communication and alignment.
➤ Quality and efficiency: Agile integrates testing and feedback throughout the development process, ensuring high quality and efficiency.

By understanding and implementing Agile SDLC, software development managers can lead their teams to deliver high-quality products that meet user needs and adapt to changing requirements. Agile provides a structured yet flexible approach that enhances collaboration, productivity, and continuous improvement.

3.2. Agile, Scrum, SAFe & other methodologies

In the dynamic world of software development, choosing the right methodology is crucial for project success. Different methodologies offer various frameworks and practices to manage and deliver software projects effectively. This chapter explores Agile, Scrum, SAFe, and other popular methodologies, highlighting their key principles, benefits, and applications.

Agile methodology

Agile is a flexible and iterative approach to software development that emphasizes collaboration, customer feedback, and continuous improvement. Key principles of Agile include:

➢ Iterative development: Breaking down projects into small, manageable increments called iterations or sprints. Each iteration delivers a potentially shippable product increment.
➢ Customer collaboration: Engaging customers and stakeholders throughout the development process to gather feedback and ensure the product meets their needs.
➢ Responding to change: Embracing changes in requirements, even late in the development process. Agile teams adapt to evolving needs and priorities.
➢ Continuous improvement: Regularly reflecting on processes and practices to identify areas for improvement. Agile promotes a culture of learning and adaptation.

Scrum framework

Scrum is a popular Agile framework that provides a structured approach to managing and delivering projects. Key components of Scrum include:

➢ Roles: Scrum defines three key roles: Product Owner, Scrum Master, and Development Team. The Product Owner prioritizes the backlog, the Scrum Master facilitates the process, and the Development Team delivers the product increment.

- ➢ Artifacts: Scrum uses artifacts such as the Product Backlog, Sprint Backlog, and Increment to manage work and track progress.
- ➢ Events: Scrum includes events like Sprint Planning, Daily Stand-ups, Sprint Review, and Sprint Retrospective. These events provide structure and ensure regular communication and feedback.
- ➢ Sprints: Scrum projects are divided into time-boxed iterations called sprints, typically lasting 2-4 weeks. Each sprint aims to deliver a potentially shippable product increment.

I recommend Scrum for companies or projects involving up to four teams working on software development projects.

Scaled Agile Framework (SAFe)

SAFe is a framework designed to scale Agile practices across large enterprises. It provides a structured approach to implementing Agile at scale, with multiple teams working together. Key elements of SAFe include:

- ➢ Levels: SAFe operates at multiple levels, including Team, Program, Large Solution, and Portfolio. Each level has specific roles, artifacts, and events.
- ➢ Agile Release Train (ART): ART is a long-lived team of Agile teams that work together to deliver value. It aligns teams to a common mission and cadence.
- ➢ PI Planning: Program Increment (PI) Planning is a key event in SAFe, where all teams come together to plan and align on objectives for the next increment.
- ➢ Lean-Agile Principles: SAFe incorporates Lean principles to optimize flow, reduce waste, and deliver value efficiently.

I recommend SAFe for companies or projects starting from five teams working on software development projects. SAFe works best in a corporate setup when many teams are working on software development projects across multiple streams.

Kanban

> Visual management: Kanban uses visual boards to manage work and track progress. Tasks are represented as cards that move through columns representing different stages of the workflow.

> Continuous flow: Unlike time-boxed iterations, Kanban focuses on continuous delivery and flow of work. Teams pull tasks as capacity allows.
> Work in Progress (WIP) limits: Kanban sets limits on the number of tasks in each stage to prevent bottlenecks and ensure smooth flow.

I recommend Kanban for DevOps teams, maintenance teams, and teams focusing on support.

By understanding the principles and practices of various methodologies, software development managers can choose the most appropriate approach for their projects. This ensures that teams can deliver high-quality products efficiently and effectively, meeting the needs of stakeholders and adapting to changing requirements.

3.3. Process improvement and optimization

Continuous process improvement and optimization are essential for maintaining efficiency, quality, and competitiveness in software development. By regularly evaluating and refining processes, teams can identify areas for enhancement, reduce waste, and deliver better products. This chapter explores strategies and best practices for process improvement and optimization in software development.

Understanding process improvement

Process improvement involves systematically identifying, analyzing, and enhancing existing processes to achieve better outcomes. Key objectives include:

➢ Increasing efficiency: Streamlining processes to reduce time, effort, and resources required to complete tasks.
➢ Enhancing quality: Improving processes to deliver higher-quality products with fewer defects and issues.
➢ Reducing waste: Eliminating non-value-added activities and inefficiencies that do not contribute to the final product.
➢ Boosting productivity: Optimizing processes to enable teams to work more effectively and achieve higher output.

3.3.1. Key steps in process improvement

Identify areas for improvement

➢ Process mapping: Create detailed maps of current processes to visualize workflows and identify bottlenecks, redundancies, and inefficiencies.
➢ Data collection: Gather data on process performance, including metrics such as cycle time, defect rates, and resource utilization. Use this data to identify areas that need improvement.

> Stakeholder feedback: Collect feedback from team members, stakeholders, and customers to understand pain points and areas for enhancement.

Analyze processes

> Root cause analysis: Conduct root cause analysis to identify the underlying causes of process inefficiencies and issues. Techniques such as the "5 Whys" and fishbone diagrams can be useful.
> Benchmarking: Compare current processes with industry best practices and standards. Identify gaps and opportunities for improvement.

Develop improvement strategies

> Set goals and objectives: Define clear and measurable goals for process improvement. Ensure that these goals align with overall business objectives.
> Brainstorm solutions: Collaborate with the team to brainstorm potential solutions and improvements. Encourage creative thinking and consider multiple approaches.
> Prioritize initiatives: Prioritize improvement initiatives based on their potential impact, feasibility, and alignment with goals.

Implement changes

> Plan implementation: Develop a detailed implementation plan that outlines the steps, resources, and timeline for executing improvements.
> Pilot testing: Conduct pilot tests to validate the effectiveness of proposed changes. Gather feedback and adjust as needed.
> Full implementation: Roll out improvements across the organization. Ensure that all team members are trained and informed about the changes.

Monitor and evaluate

➢ Track performance: Continuously monitor process performance using key metrics and indicators. Compare results against goals to assess the effectiveness of improvements.

➢ Gather feedback: Collect feedback from team members and stakeholders to identify any issues or areas for further improvement.

➢ Iterate and refine: Use the feedback and performance data to make iterative refinements. Continuously seek opportunities for further optimization.

3.3.2. Best practices for process optimization

Adopt Agile Practices

➢ Iterative development: Implement iterative development practices, such as Agile and Scrum, to enable continuous improvement and adaptability.

➢ Regular retrospectives: Conduct regular retrospectives to reflect on processes, identify areas for improvement, and implement changes.

Implement lean principles

➢ Value stream mapping: Use value stream mapping to visualize and analyze the flow of value through processes. Identify and eliminate waste to optimize flow.

➢ Continuous improvement (Kaizen): Foster a culture of continuous improvement (Kaizen) where team members are encouraged to suggest and implement small, incremental changes.

Leverage automation

➢ Automate repetitive tasks: Implement automation tools to handle repetitive and manual tasks, such as testing, deployment, and code integration. This reduces errors and frees up time for more valuable activities.

➢ Continuous integration and deployment (CI/CD): Adopt CI/CD practices to automate the build, testing, and deployment processes. This ensures faster and more reliable delivery of software.

➢ DevSecOps: Implement cybersecurity in your automation and automate SAST (Static Application Security Testing) and DAST (Dynamic Application Security Testing) in your CI/CD.

Enhance collaboration and communication

➢ Cross-Functional teams: Build cross-functional teams with diverse skills and perspectives. This enhances collaboration and problem-solving.

➢ Effective communication tools: Use communication tools and platforms to facilitate real-time collaboration and information sharing.

Focus on quality

➢ Quality assurance practices: Implement robust quality assurance practices, including automated testing, code reviews, and peer programming.

➢ Customer feedback: Continuously gather and incorporate customer feedback to ensure that the product meets user needs and expectations.

Measure and analyze performance

➢ Key Performance Indicators (KPIs): Define and track KPIs to measure process performance. Use these metrics to identify trends, assess progress, and make data-driven decisions.

➢ Data-driven decision making: Use data and analytics to inform process improvement initiatives. Analyze performance data to identify patterns and areas for optimization.

3.3.3. Challenges in process improvement

Process improvement can encounter various challenges, including resistance to change, limited resources, and conflicting priorities. Strategies to overcome these challenges include:

➢ Change management: Implement effective change management practices to address resistance and ensure smooth adoption of improvements. Communicate the benefits and involve team members in the process.
➢ Resource allocation: Allocate sufficient resources, including time, budget, and personnel, to support process improvement initiatives. Prioritize initiatives based on their potential impact.
➢ Stakeholder engagement: Engage stakeholders throughout the process to ensure alignment and support. Regularly communicate progress and gather feedback.

By continuously improving and optimizing processes, software development teams can enhance efficiency, quality, and productivity. These practices not only lead to better project outcomes but also foster a culture of innovation and excellence.

3.4. Quality assurance and testing in Agile

Quality assurance (QA) and testing are integral parts of the Agile development process. Agile methodologies emphasize continuous testing and feedback to ensure that the software meets user needs and maintains high quality throughout its lifecycle. This chapter explores the principles, practices, and strategies for effective QA and testing in Agile environments.

Principles of agile QA and testing

Agile QA and testing are guided by several key principles:

- ➢ Continuous testing: Testing is performed continuously throughout the development process, rather than being a separate phase at the end. This helps identify and address issues early.
- ➢ Collaboration: QA and testing are collaborative efforts involving the entire team, including developers, testers, and stakeholders. This ensures that quality is a shared responsibility.
- ➢ Customer focus: Testing is driven by user stories and acceptance criteria, ensuring that the software meets customer needs and expectations.
- ➢ Automation: Automated testing is extensively utilized to increase efficiency, reduce manual effort, and ensure consistent test coverage. Agile cannot exist without automation testing.
- ➢ Iterative improvement: Testing practices are continuously refined and improved based on feedback and lessons learned from each iteration.

3.4.1. Key practices in Agile QA and testing

Test-Driven Development (TDD)

- ➢ Writing tests first: In TDD, tests are written before the code. This ensures that the code meets the specified requirements and helps prevent defects.
- ➢ Red-green-refactor cycle: The TDD process follows a cycle of writing a failing test (red), writing code to pass

the test (green), and then refactoring the code for optimization.

Behavior-Driven Development (BDD)

➤ Defining behavior: BDD focuses on defining the behavior of the software in terms of user stories and acceptance criteria. Tests are written in a natural language format that is understandable by all stakeholders.

➤ Collaboration: BDD encourages collaboration between developers, testers, and business stakeholders to ensure that the software meets business requirements.

Automated testing

➤ Unit testing: Automated unit tests verify the functionality of individual components or units of code. These tests are typically written by developers and run frequently.

➤ Integration testing: Automated integration tests ensure that different components of the software work together as expected. These tests validate the interactions between modules.

➤ End-to-End testing: Automated end-to-end tests simulate user interactions with the software to verify that the entire system functions correctly. These tests cover user workflows and scenarios.

Use AI tools to help you write tests and speed up the process. In my practice, most unit tests are written with the help of AI tools.

Continuous integration (CI)

➤ Frequent integration: CI involves integrating code changes frequently, often multiple times a day. This helps detect and resolve integration issues early.

➤ Automated builds and tests: CI systems automatically build the software and run tests whenever code changes

are integrated. This ensures that the software remains stable and functional.
- ➢ Nightly test: Use nightly pipelines to run extensive regression tests during the night to get the output for analysis the next day.

Exploratory testing (smoke tests)

- ➢ Ad-hoc testing: Exploratory testing involves ad-hoc, unscripted testing to discover defects and issues that may not be covered by automated tests. Testers use their creativity and intuition to explore the software.
- ➢ Learning and adaptation: Exploratory testing is iterative and adaptive. Testers learn about the software as they test and adjust their approach based on their findings.

Acceptance testing

- ➢ User Acceptance Testing (UAT): UAT involves end-users testing the software to ensure that it meets their needs and expectations. This helps ensure that the software is ready for production.
- ➢ Acceptance criteria: Acceptance tests are based on predefined acceptance criteria that define the conditions under which a user story is considered complete.

3.4.2. Strategies for effective Agile QA & testing

Early and continuous involvement

- ➢ Involve QA early: Involve QA and testing activities from the beginning of the project. This ensures that quality considerations are integrated into the development process.
- ➢ Continuous feedback: Provide continuous feedback to developers based on test results. This helps identify and address issues promptly.

Collaboration and communication

➢ Cross-functional teams: Build cross-functional teams that include developers, testers, and business stakeholders. This enhances collaboration and ensures that quality is a shared responsibility.
➢ Regular meetings: Conduct regular meetings, such as daily stand-ups and sprint reviews, to discuss progress, issues, and testing activities.

Test automation

➢ Automate repetitive tests: Automate repetitive and time-consuming tests to increase efficiency and reduce manual effort. Focus on automating unit, integration, and end-to-end tests.
➢ Maintain test suites: Regularly update and maintain automated test suites to ensure that they remain relevant and effective.

Continuous improvement

➢ Retrospectives: Conduct regular retrospectives to reflect on testing practices and identify areas for improvement. Implement changes based on feedback and lessons learned.
➢ Learning and development: Encourage continuous learning and development for QA team members. Provide access to training, workshops, and conferences.

Risk-based testing

➢ Prioritize testing: Prioritize testing activities based on risk. Focus on testing the most critical and high-risk areas of the software first. This is essential when developing software for regulated industries like the life sciences sector.

➤ Risk assessment: Conduct risk assessments to identify potential issues and their impact. Use this information to guide testing efforts.

3.4.3. Benefits of Agile QA & testing

Agile QA and testing offer several benefits:

➤ Early detection of issues: Continuous testing helps identify and address issues early in the development process, reducing the cost and effort of fixing defects.
➤ Improved collaboration: Agile promotes collaboration between developers, testers, and stakeholders, leading to better communication and alignment.
➤ Higher quality: Regular testing and feedback ensure that the software meets quality standards and user expectations.
➤ Faster delivery: Automated testing and continuous integration enable faster and more reliable delivery of software.
➤ Adaptability: Agile QA and testing practices are flexible and adaptable, allowing teams to respond to changing requirements and priorities.

By implementing effective QA and testing practices in Agile environments, software development teams can ensure that their products are of high quality, meet user needs, and are delivered efficiently. Continuous testing and feedback are key to maintaining quality and achieving successful project outcomes.

3.5. Continuous integration & deployment

Continuous Integration (CI) and Continuous Deployment (CD) are fundamental practices in Agile development that enable teams to deliver high-quality software quickly and reliably. CI/CD automates the integration, testing, and deployment processes, ensuring that code changes are continuously validated and deployed. This chapter explores the principles, practices, and tools for implementing CI/CD in Agile environments.

Principles of CI/CD in Agile

CI/CD embodies several key principles that align with Agile methodologies:

➢ Frequent integration: Developers frequently merge code changes into a central repository. This practice helps avoid integration challenges and ensures that the codebase remains stable.
➢ Automated testing: Automated tests are run against the integrated code to validate changes and detect issues early. This ensures that the application is not broken whenever new commits are integrated.
➢ Continuous delivery: Code changes are automatically deployed to testing and production environments after passing automated tests. This enables teams to release software frequently and reliably.
➢ Continuous deployment: Every change that passes all stages of the CI/CD pipeline is automatically deployed to production. This practice accelerates the feedback loop and allows teams to focus on building software.

Benefits of CI/CD in Agile

CI/CD offers several benefits that enhance Agile development:

➢ Faster delivery: CI/CD automates the integration, testing, and deployment processes, enabling teams to deliver software quickly and reliably.

- ➤ Improved quality: Automated testing ensures that code changes are continuously validated, reducing the risk of defects and improving software quality.
- ➤ Enhanced collaboration: CI/CD fosters collaboration among team members by providing a consistent and automated process for integrating and deploying code changes.
- ➤ Reduced risk: Frequent integration and automated testing help detect and resolve issues early, reducing the risk of conflicts and integration challenges.
- ➤ Continuous feedback: Continuous deployment accelerates the feedback loop, allowing teams to gather user feedback and make improvements quickly.

Conclusion

Implementing CI/CD in Agile development enhances collaboration, quality, and delivery speed. By automating the integration, testing, and deployment processes, Agile teams can deliver high-quality software that meets user needs and adapts to changing requirements. Understanding and leveraging CI/CD practices and tools is essential for successful Agile development and continuous improvement.

3.6. Measuring team performance in Agile

Measuring team performance in Agile environments is crucial for ensuring continuous improvement and delivering high-quality products. Agile methodologies emphasize flexibility, collaboration, and iterative progress, making traditional performance metrics less effective. Instead, Agile teams rely on a variety of specialized metrics to gauge their efficiency, predictability, and overall health.

Key metrics:

➢ Velocity: This measures the amount of work a team completes during a sprint, usually in story points. It's important for tracking progress over time, but it shouldn't be used to compare different teams because each team may estimate story points differently.

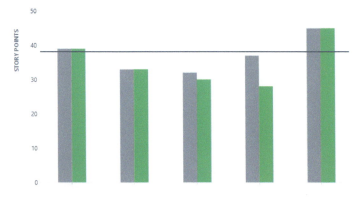

➢ Predictability: This metric compares the number of user stories a team commits to at the beginning of a sprint with the number of stories they complete. High predictability indicates that a team is good at planning and delivering on their commitments.
➢ Cumulative flow diagram (CFD): A visual tool that shows the status of work items over time. It helps teams understand workflow, identify bottlenecks, and improve processes by showing the amount of work in different stages (e.g., to-do, in progress, done).

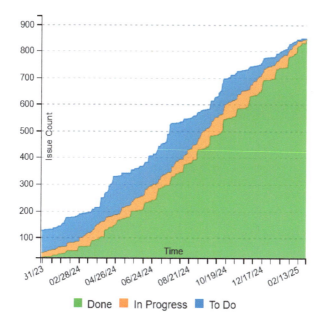

Done   In Progress   To Do

➢ Backlog health monitoring: This involves regularly reviewing the backlog to ensure it is well-groomed, prioritized, and contains enough ready-to-work items. A healthy backlog helps teams maintain a steady flow of work

105
Total

🔴 **17**
No estimates

0
Not defined - description

⚠️ **15**
Not defined - acceptance criteria

⚠️ **25**
No priority

⚠️ **28**
Not assigned

➢ Teams' sprint health: Shows how the sprint is progressing by indicating how much work is not started, how much is in progress, and how many story points are completed, considering the number of days left in the sprint

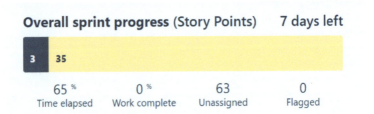

Overall sprint progress (Story Points)   **7 days left**

3	35		

65 %	0 %	63	0
Time elapsed	Work complete	Unassigned	Flagged

➢ Burndown chart: A graphical representation of work left to do versus time. It shows the progress of a sprint and helps teams see if they are on track to complete their work by the end of the sprint.

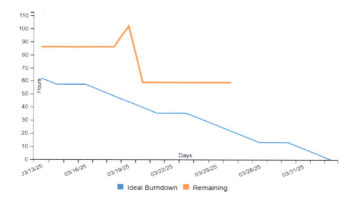

➤ Release burnup chart: This chart tracks progress towards a release goal. It shows the amount of work completed over time and helps teams understand how close they are to delivering a release. It can also highlight scope changes and their impact on the release timeline

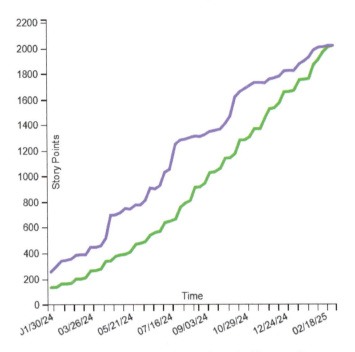

Here are some additional popular Agile performance metrics:

➢ Lead time: Measures the total time from when a task is requested to when it is completed. Shorter lead times indicate efficient processes and quick delivery of value to customers.

➢ Cycle time: Tracks the time it takes to complete a task once work has started. Reducing cycle time helps streamline workflows and improve productivity.

➢ Throughput: The number of tasks completed in a specific period. This metric helps teams understand their capacity and optimize their workflow.

➢ Defect density: Measures the number of defects per unit of work (e.g., per story point or per sprint). Lower defect density indicates higher quality and fewer issues in the delivered product.

- ➢ Customer satisfaction: Often measured through surveys or feedback forms, this metric gauge how satisfied customers are with the product or service delivered. High customer satisfaction indicates that the team is meeting or exceeding customer expectations.
- ➢ Team morale: Assessed through regular surveys or check-ins, this metric helps understand the team's overall well-being and satisfaction. High morale is crucial for maintaining productivity and a positive work environment.
- ➢ Work in progress (WIP): The number of tasks currently being worked on. Keeping WIP limits helps prevent bottlenecks and ensures that the team is focused on completing tasks efficiently.

4. Tools

4.1. Essential tools for software development

Agile development emphasizes collaboration, flexibility, and continuous delivery. To support these principles, teams rely on a variety of tools that streamline processes, enhance communication, and improve productivity. This chapter explores essential tools for software development in the context of Agile, covering project management, version control, continuous integration, testing, and collaboration.

4.1.1. Integrated development environments

Integrated Development Environments (IDEs) are powerful tools that streamline the software development process by providing comprehensive facilities to programmers for software development. These environments are designed to enhance productivity by integrating various development tools into a single application. An IDE typically consists of a source code editor, build automation tools, and a debugger, but often includes many other features such as version control integration, code navigation, and testing tools.

The source code editor is the core component of an IDE, offering syntax highlighting, code completion, and error detection to help developers write code more efficiently. Build automation tools simplify the process of compiling and linking code, reducing the time and effort required to produce executable programs. The debugger allows developers to inspect the state of their applications at runtime, set breakpoints, and step through code to identify and fix bugs.

Two of the most popular IDEs in the industry today are Visual Studio and IntelliJ IDEA. These IDEs are renowned for their robust feature sets, user-friendly interfaces, and extensive plugin ecosystems, making them the go-to choices for many developers across various programming languages and platforms. Visual Studio, developed by Microsoft, is particularly favored for .NET and C++ development, while IntelliJ IDEA, created by JetBrains, is highly regarded among Java developers and those who appreciate its intelligent code assistance and ergonomic design.

4.1.2. Version control systems

Version control systems (VCS) are essential for managing code changes, collaborating with team members, and maintaining code integrity. Key features include branching, merging, and history tracking. Essential version control systems for Agile development include:

47

Git

➢ Distributed version control: Git is a distributed VCS that allows team members to work on code independently and merge changes seamlessly.

➢ Branching and merging: Create branches for new features, bug fixes, and experiments. Merge changes back into the main branch when ready.

➢ Commit history: Track changes with detailed commit history, making it easy to review and revert changes if needed.

➢ Collaboration: Collaborate with team members through pull requests, code reviews, and comments.

GitHub

➢ Repository hosting: Host Git repositories in the cloud, making them accessible to team members from anywhere.

➢ Pull requests: Use pull requests to review and discuss code changes before merging them into the main branch.

➢ Issues and projects: Track bugs, feature requests, and tasks using GitHub issues and projects.

➢ Integrations: Integrate GitHub with CI/CD tools, project management tools, and other services to streamline workflows.

GitLab

➢ Integrated CI/CD: GitLab provides integrated CI/CD pipelines to automate testing and deployment.

➢ Repository management: Manage Git repositories with features like branching, merging, and access control.

➢ Issue tracking: Track issues, plan sprints, and manage projects using GitLab's built-in tools.

➢ Collaboration: Collaborate with team members through merge requests, code reviews, and comments.

4.1.3. CI/CD tools

CI/CD tools automate the build, testing, and deployment processes, enabling Agile teams to deliver software quickly and reliably. Essential CI/CD tools for Agile development include:

Jenkins

Automation Server: Jenkins is an open-source automation server that supports building, testing, and deploying code.

➤ Pipeline as Code: Define CI/CD pipelines as code using Jenkinsfile, allowing version control and easy updates.
➤ Plugins: Extend Jenkins functionality with a wide range of plugins for different tools and technologies.

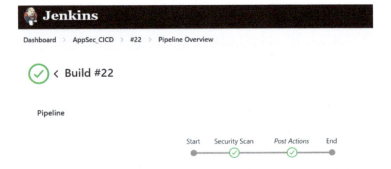

Azure DevOps

➤ Azure pipelines: Build, test, and deploy with CI/CD that works with any language, platform, and cloud.
➤ Integration: Seamlessly integrate with GitHub, Jenkins, and other tools to enhance collaboration and productivity.

#20241203.1 • Merged PR 37: Finish sprint 11
Individual CI for (AK) master ↟ 62dfff76

#20241105.1 • Update azure-pipelines.yml for Azure Pipelines
Individual CI for (AK) master ↟ 698c7881

#20241104.1 • Merged PR 36: Sprint 9 end
Individual CI for (AK) master ↟ 2f4e544f

GitLab CI/CD

➢ Integrated CI/CD: GitLab provides integrated CI/CD pipelines to automate testing and deployment.
➢ Repository management: Manage Git repositories with features like branching, merging, and access control.

4.1.4. Testing tools

Testing tools are essential for ensuring the quality and reliability of software. They support various types of testing, including unit, integration, and end-to-end testing. Essential testing tools for Agile development include:

Selenium

➢ Web testing: Selenium is an open-source tool for automating web browser testing, with the capability to integrate with all common programming languages.
➢ Cross-browser testing: Test web applications across different browsers and platforms.
➢ Integration: Integrate Selenium with CI/CD tools to automate testing as part of the build process.

NUnit

➤ Unit testing for .NET: NUnit is a widely used framework for writing and running unit tests in .NET applications.

MSTest

➤ Unit testing for .NET: MSTest is a unit testing framework provided by Microsoft, integrated with Visual Studio.

JUnit

➤ JUnit Testing for Java: JUnit is a testing framework offering advanced features like parameterization and parallel execution.

Spock Framework

➤ Testing for Java and Groovy: Spock is a testing and specification framework for Java and Groovy applications, combining features of JUnit, TestNG, and Mockito.

4.1.5. Mocking tools

Mocking tools are essential in unit testing as they allow developers to simulate the behavior of complex dependencies and isolate the code under test. By creating mock objects, developers can focus on testing the functionality of a specific unit without being affected by external systems or components.

Key features of mocking tools

➤ Isolation of code: Mocking tools help isolate the code under test by replacing real dependencies with mock objects. This ensures that tests are focused solely on the unit being tested, leading to more accurate and reliable results.
➤ Simulating behavior: Mock objects can simulate the behavior of real objects, including their methods and properties. This allows developers to test how the unit

interacts with its dependencies under various conditions.

➤ Control over test environment: Mocking tools provide control over the test environment by allowing developers to define the behavior of mock objects. This includes specifying return values, throwing exceptions, and verifying method calls.

➤ Improved test coverage: By using mock objects, developers can create tests for scenarios that are difficult or impossible to reproduce with real dependencies. This leads to improved test coverage and more robust code.

Faster test execution: Mocking tools can speed up test execution by eliminating the need to interact with slow or resource-intensive dependencies. This results in faster feedback and more efficient development cycles.

Popular mocking tools

➤ Mockito: A popular mocking framework for Java, Mockito allows developers to create mock objects and define their behavior using a simple and intuitive API.

➤ Jest: A JavaScript testing framework that includes built-in mocking capabilities, making it easy to create mock objects and functions for unit tests.

➤ Moq: A widely used mocking library for .NET, Moq provides a fluent API for creating and configuring mock objects.

➤ Pytest-mock: An extension for the Pytest framework in Python, Pytest-mock simplifies the creation of mock objects and their integration into unit tests.

Benefits of using mocking tools in Unit Testing

➤ Increased reliability: By isolating the code under test, mocking tools help ensure that unit tests are reliable and not affected by external factors.

➤ Simplified testing: Mocking tools simplify the process of writing unit tests by providing a way to simulate complex dependencies and control their behavior.
➤ Enhanced debugging: Mock objects can help identify issues in the code by allowing developers to test specific interactions and verify the expected behavior.
➤ Cost efficiency: Mocking tools reduce the need for setting up and maintaining real dependencies, leading to cost savings in terms of time and resources.

4.1.6. Collaboration and communication tools

Effective collaboration and communication are crucial for Agile teams. These tools facilitate real-time communication, file sharing, and collaboration. Essential collaboration and communication tools for Agile development include:

Slack

➤ Real-time messaging: Slack provides real-time messaging and collaboration for teams.
➤ Channels: Organize conversations into channels based on projects, topics, or teams.
➤ Integrations: Integrate Slack with project management, CI/CD, and other tools to receive notifications and updates.

Microsoft Teams

➤ Team collaboration: Microsoft Teams offers chat, video conferencing, and file sharing for team collaboration.
➤ Channels and tabs: Organize conversations into channels and add tabs for quick access to tools and documents.
➤ Integrations: Integrate Microsoft Teams with project management, CI/CD, and other tools to streamline workflows.

Confluence

- ➤ Documentation and collaboration: Confluence is a collaboration tool for creating, sharing, and managing documentation.
- ➤ Spaces and pages: Organize content into spaces and pages for easy navigation and access.
- ➤ Integration: Integrate confluence with Jira, Slack.

4.2. Project management software

Project management software plays a crucial role in Agile development by helping teams plan, track, and manage their work efficiently. These tools support Agile methodologies such as Scrum and Kanban, enabling teams to collaborate effectively, visualize progress, and adapt to changes. This chapter explores various project management software options that are specifically designed for Agile development, highlighting their key features and benefits.

Jira

Jira is one of the most popular project management tools for Agile teams. Developed by Atlassian, Jira supports both Scrum and Kanban methodologies and offers a wide range of features to manage Agile projects.

➤ Backlog management: Create and prioritize user stories, tasks, and bugs in the product backlog.
➤ Sprint planning: Plan and manage sprints, assign tasks, and set sprint goals.
➤ Kanban and scrum boards: Visualize work using customizable Kanban and Scrum boards to track progress and identify bottlenecks.
➤ Reporting and analytics: Generate detailed reports and analytics to monitor team performance and project status.
➤ Integrations: Integrate with other tools such as Confluence, Bitbucket, and Slack to streamline workflows.

Azure DevOps

Azure DevOps by Microsoft is a comprehensive suite of development tools that supports Agile project management, continuous integration, and continuous delivery.

➤ Azure boards: Track work with configurable Kanban boards, interactive backlogs, and powerful planning tools with unparalleled traceability.
➤ Azure pipelines: Build, test, and deploy with CI/CD that works with any language, platform, and cloud.
➤ Azure repos: Collaborate to build better code with pull requests and advanced file management with unlimited, cloud-hosted private Git repos.
➤ Azure test plans: Test and ship with confidence using manual and exploratory testing tools.
➤ Integration: Seamlessly integrate with GitHub, Jenkins, and other tools to enhance collaboration and productivity.

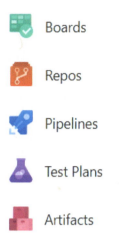

Boards

Repos

Pipelines

Test Plans

Artifacts

Jira Align

Jira Align supports SAFe by providing a centralized platform for aligning strategy with execution, improving visibility, and fostering collaboration. Key features:

➢ Unified workspace: Provides a single platform for aligning strategy with execution, ensuring all teams are on the same page
➢ Reporting and dashboards: Offers real-time reporting and configurable dashboards to track progress and performance across the organization
➢ Flow metrics: Helps improve the flow of value by providing insights into bottlenecks and inefficiencies.
➢ OKR management: Facilitates the setting and tracking of objectives and key results to ensure alignment with strategic goals
➢ Seamless integration: Integrates with popular CI/CD tools to automate workflows and enhance efficiency
➢ Strategy pyramid: Links mission, vision, and values to goals and objectives, promoting alignment and collaboration

> Data-driven decisions: Provides enterprise insights to support data-driven decision-making and continuous improvement

Conclusion

Selecting the right project management software is crucial for Agile teams to effectively plan, track, and manage their work. Tools like Jira, Azure DevOps, Jira Align offer a range of features that support Agile methodologies and enhance collaboration, productivity, and efficiency. By leveraging these tools, Agile teams can deliver high-quality software that meets user needs and adapts to changing requirements.

4.3. Version control systems

Version control systems (VCS) are fundamental to Agile development, enabling teams to manage code changes, collaborate effectively, and maintain code integrity. This chapter explores the role of version control systems in Agile development, highlighting their benefits, types, and best practices.

The role of version control in Agile

Version control is essential for Agile practices, supporting continuous integration, collaboration, and iterative development. Key roles of VCS in Agile include:

> Managing code changes: VCS tracks changes to the codebase, allowing multiple developers to work on the same project without conflicts. It provides a history of changes, making it easy to revert to previous versions if needed.
> Facilitating collaboration: VCS enables team members to work concurrently on different features or bug fixes.

Branching and merging capabilities allow developers to isolate their work and integrate it seamlessly.

➢ Supporting continuous integration: VCS integrates with CI/CD tools to automate the build, testing, and deployment processes. This ensures that code changes are continuously tested and integrated, reducing the risk of integration issues

4.3.1. Best practices for using version control

To maximize the benefits of version control in Agile development, teams should follow these best practices:

Branching strategies

➢ Feature branching: Create separate branches for each feature or bug fix. This allows developers to work independently and merge changes back into the main branch when ready.

➢ Release branching: Create branches for different releases to manage and maintain multiple versions of the software.

➢ Trunk-based development: Keep the main branch (trunk) stable and integrate changes frequently. This reduces the risk of long-lived branches and complex merges.

Commit practices

➢ Frequent commits: Commit changes frequently to keep the codebase up-to-date and reduce the risk of conflicts.

➢ Descriptive commit messages: Write clear and descriptive commit messages to explain the purpose of each change. This helps team members understand the history and context of changes.

> Small, atomic commits: Make small, atomic commits that focus on a single task or change. This makes it easier to review and revert changes if needed.

Code reviews

> Peer reviews: Conduct peer reviews for all code changes before merging them into the main branch. This helps identify issues early and ensures code quality.
> Pull requests: Use pull requests to facilitate code reviews and discussions. Reviewers can provide feedback, suggest improvements, and approve changes before they are merged.

Continuous integration

> Automated builds and tests: Integrate VCS with CI tools to automate the build and testing processes. This ensures that code changes are continuously tested and integrated.
> Frequent integration: Integrate changes frequently to detect and resolve integration issues early. This reduces the risk of conflicts and ensures a stable codebase.

Documentation and training

> Version control policies: Establish clear version control policies and guidelines for the team. This includes branching strategies, commit practices, and code review processes.
> Training and onboarding: Provide training and onboarding for new team members to ensure they understand and follow version control practices.

Conclusion

Version control systems are indispensable for Agile development, enabling teams to manage code changes, collaborate effectively, and maintain code integrity. By following best practices and leveraging the capabilities of tools like Git, Agile teams can enhance their development processes, reduce risks, and deliver high-quality software. Understanding the role and benefits of version control in Agile is essential for successful project management and continuous improvement.

5. Delivery

5.1. Planning and estimation in Agile

Planning and estimation are crucial components of Agile development, enabling teams to deliver high-quality software efficiently and predictably. Agile methodologies emphasize flexibility, collaboration, and iterative progress, which require effective planning and accurate estimation. This chapter explores the principles, techniques, and best practices for planning and estimation in Agile environments.

Principles of Agile planning and estimation

Agile planning and estimation are guided by several key principles:

➤ Iterative planning: Agile planning is iterative and ongoing, allowing teams to adapt to changes and refine plans based on feedback and evolving requirements.
➤ Collaborative approach: Planning and estimation involve collaboration among team members, stakeholders, and customers to ensure alignment and shared understanding.
➤ Relative estimation: Agile estimation uses relative sizing to compare the complexity and effort of different tasks, rather than absolute time estimates.

➢ Flexibility and adaptability: Agile plans are flexible and can be adjusted based on new information, changing priorities, and feedback.

5.1.1. Agile planning techniques

Sprint planning

➢ Purpose: Sprint planning is a collaborative meeting where the team defines the work to be completed in the upcoming sprint. It sets clear goals and priorities for the sprint.
➢ Process: The Product Owner presents the prioritized backlog items, and the team discusses and selects items to work on. The team estimates the effort required and commits to completing the selected items.
➢ Outcome: A sprint backlog with clearly defined tasks and goals for the sprint.

Backlog grooming /refinement

➢ Purpose: Backlog grooming (or refinement) is an ongoing process where the team reviews and updates the product backlog to ensure it is well-defined and prioritized.
➢ Process: The team discusses backlog items, clarifies requirements, and estimates effort. Items are prioritized based on business value and readiness for development.
➢ Outcome: A refined and prioritized backlog that is ready for sprint planning.

Release planning

➢ Purpose: Release planning involves defining the scope and timeline for a release, aligning it with business goals and stakeholder expectations.

> Process: The team collaborates with stakeholders to identify key features and milestones for the release. The team estimates effort and defines a release plan with target dates.
> Outcome: A release plan with defined scope, milestones, and timelines.

5.1.2. Agile estimation techniques

Planning poker

> Purpose: Planning poker is a collaborative estimation technique that uses consensus to estimate the effort required for backlog items.
> Process: Team members use numbered cards to estimate the effort for a backlog item. They discuss their estimates and reach a consensus.
> Outcome: A shared understanding of the effort required for each backlog item.

Story points

> Purpose: Story points are a relative estimation technique that measures the complexity and effort of user stories.
> Process: The team assigns story points to user stories based on their complexity, risks, and effort. Story points are typically based on the Fibonacci sequence (e.g., 1, 2, 3, 5, 8, 13).
> Outcome: A set of user stories with assigned story points, providing a relative measure of effort.

T-Shirt sizes

> Purpose: T-Shirt sizes (e.g., XS, S, M, L, XL) are a simple and intuitive way to estimate the effort required for tasks.

- ➢ Process: The team categorizes tasks into T-Shirt sizes based on their complexity and effort. This technique is useful for quick and high-level estimation.
- ➢ Outcome: Tasks categorized into T-Shirt sizes, providing a relative measure of effort.

Fibonacci sequence

- ➢ Purpose: The Fibonacci sequence is used in Agile estimation to provide a realistic way for teams to forecast work.
- ➢ Process: The team uses the Fibonacci sequence (e.g., 1, 2, 3, 5, 8, 13) to estimate the effort required for tasks. This sequence creates a buffer in estimating that allows for change.
- ➢ Outcome: Tasks estimated using the Fibonacci sequence, providing a relative measure of effort.

5.1.3. Best practices for planning and estimation

Collaborative planning

- ➢ Involve the whole team: Engage the entire team in planning and estimation activities to ensure shared understanding and commitment.
- ➢ Stakeholder engagement: Collaborate with stakeholders to gather requirements, clarify priorities, and align on goals.

Continuous refinement

- ➢ Regular backlog grooming: Continuously refine the backlog to ensure it is well-defined and prioritized.
- ➢ Iterative planning: Plan iteratively, adjusting plans based on feedback and changing requirements.

Relative estimation

- Use story points: Use story points to estimate the complexity and effort of user stories, rather than absolute time estimates.
- Leverage T-Shirt sizes: Use T-Shirt sizes for quick and high-level estimation.

Transparency and communication

- Clear communication: Communicate plans, estimates, and progress clearly to the team and stakeholders.
- Regular updates: Provide regular updates on progress, changes, and challenges.

Flexibility and adaptability

- Embrace change: Be flexible and adapt plans based on new information, changing priorities, and feedback.
- Iterative improvement: Continuously improve planning and estimation practices based on lessons learned.

Conclusion

Effective planning and estimation are essential for successful Agile development. By leveraging collaborative planning techniques and relative estimation methods, Agile teams can deliver high-quality software efficiently and predictably. Understanding and implementing these principles and practices is key to achieving successful project outcomes and continuous improvement.

5.2. Managing deadlines and milestones

Managing deadlines and milestones in Agile development requires a balance between flexibility and commitment. Agile methodologies emphasize iterative progress and adaptability, but deadlines and milestones are still essential for setting expectations, tracking progress, and ensuring timely delivery. This chapter explores strategies and best practices for managing deadlines and milestones in Agile environments.

The role of deadlines in Agile

Deadlines in Agile serve several important purposes:

➢ Setting expectations: Deadlines help set clear expectations for stakeholders, team members, and customers. They provide a timeline for when features or deliverables will be completed.
➢ Driving progress: Deadlines create a sense of urgency and focus, motivating the team to work efficiently and meet their commitments.
➢ Facilitating planning: Deadlines enable better planning and coordination with other teams, departments, or external partners who may depend on the deliverables.

5.2.1. Strategies for managing deadlines

Realistic goal setting

➢ Define achievable goals: Set clear, achievable goals to prevent frustration and delays. Break down large objectives into smaller, manageable tasks with specific timelines.
➢ Prioritize core features: Focus on essential features first to ensure the project remains on track. Secondary features can be added later if time permits.

Iterative planning

➢ Sprint planning: Use sprint planning to define the work to be completed in each iteration. This helps the team focus on short-term goals while making steady progress towards the overall deadline.

> Backlog grooming: Continuously refine and prioritize the backlog to ensure that the most important tasks are addressed first.

Transparent communication

> Stakeholder engagement: Maintain transparent communication with stakeholders about project scope, timelines, and progress. This helps manage expectations and avoid scope creep.
> Regular updates: Provide regular updates on progress, changes, and challenges. This keeps everyone informed and aligned.

Resource allocation

> Assign tasks wisely: Allocate tasks based on team members' expertise and avoid overloading individuals. This helps maintain focus and speed up project execution
> Plan for contingencies: Include buffer time for testing, debugging, and unexpected issues to prevent minor setbacks from causing major delays.

The role of milestones in Agile

Milestones in Agile mark significant stages of development and help visualize progress. They act as signposts to indicate how much progress has been made and what still needs to be done

> Tracking progress: Milestones provide a way to track progress and ensure that the project is on schedule. They help identify any deviations from the plan and allow for timely adjustments.
> Celebrating achievements: Milestones offer opportunities to celebrate achievements and recognize the team's hard work. This boosts morale and motivation.

> ➢ Aligning stakeholders: Milestones help align stakeholders by providing clear points of reference for project status and progress.

5.2.2. Strategies for managing milestones

Define clear milestones

> ➢ Specific and measurable: Define milestones that are specific and measurable. This ensures that progress can be tracked accurately.
> ➢ Aligned with goals: Ensure that milestones align with the overall project goals and deliverables. This keeps the team focused on the most important outcomes.

Regular review and adjustment

> ➢ Review progress: Regularly review progress towards milestones during sprint reviews and retrospectives. This helps identify any issues or delays early.
> ➢ Adjust plans: Be flexible and adjust plans based on progress and feedback. This ensures that the project remains on track and adapts to changing requirements.

Celebrate achievements

> ➢ Recognize success: Celebrate the achievement of milestones to recognize the team's hard work and boost morale.
> ➢ Reflect and learn: Use milestone achievements as opportunities to reflect on what went well and what can be improved. This promotes continuous improvement.

Conclusion

Managing deadlines and milestones in Agile development requires a balance between flexibility and commitment. By setting realistic goals, engaging stakeholders, and

67

continuously reviewing progress, Agile teams can effectively manage deadlines and milestones to ensure timely delivery and high-quality outcomes. Understanding and implementing these strategies is key to achieving successful project management and continuous improvement in Agile environments.

5.3. Risk management

Risk management is a critical aspect of Agile development, enabling teams to identify, assess, and mitigate risks continuously throughout the project lifecycle. Agile methodologies, with their iterative and adaptive nature, provide unique opportunities to focus on testing what is most important to manage risks effectively. This chapter explores the principles, practices, and strategies for risk management in Agile, emphasizing the importance of testing.

Principles of agile risk management

Agile risk management is guided by several key principles:

➤ Continuous risk identification: Risks are identified continuously throughout the project, allowing teams to respond to new risks as they emerge.

➤ Collaborative approach: Risk management involves the entire team, including developers, testers, and stakeholders, ensuring that all perspectives are considered.

➤ Iterative risk assessment: Risks are assessed iteratively, with regular reviews and updates to prioritize risks based on their potential impact and likelihood.

➤ Adaptive risk response: Agile teams adapt their risk responses based on changing project conditions and feedback, ensuring that mitigation strategies remain effective.

5.3.1. Focusing on testing what is important

Effective risk management in Agile requires a focus on testing what is most important. This involves prioritizing tests based on the potential impact of risks and ensuring that critical areas are thoroughly validated.

Risk-based testing

➢ Identify high-risk areas: Use risk analysis to identify high-risk areas of the software. These may include complex features, critical functionalities, or areas with a history of issues.
➢ Prioritize tests: Prioritize testing efforts based on the identified risks. Focus on testing high-risk areas first to ensure that critical issues are detected and addressed early.

Test automation

➢ Automate high-risk tests: Implement automated tests for high-risk areas to ensure consistent and thorough validation. Automated tests can be run frequently to detect issues early.
➢ Continuous integration: Integrate automated tests into the CI/CD pipeline to ensure that high-risk areas are continuously tested whenever code changes are made.

Exploratory testing

➢ Ad-hoc testing: Use exploratory testing to investigate high-risk areas in an unscripted manner. Testers use their creativity and intuition to explore the software and identify potential issues.

> Focus on critical paths: During exploratory testing, focus on critical user paths and scenarios that are most likely to be affected by risks.

Regression testing

> Validate changes: Implement regression testing to validate that recent changes have not introduced new issues. Focus on high-risk areas to ensure that critical functionalities remain intact.
> Automate regression tests: Use automated regression tests to ensure consistent validation of high-risk areas whenever changes are made.

Benefits of risk-based testing in Agile

Risk-based testing offers several benefits that enhance Agile risk management:

> Proactive risk identification: Continuous testing helps identify and address risks early, reducing the likelihood of issues escalating.
> Improved quality: Focusing on high-risk areas ensures that critical functionalities are thoroughly validated, improving overall software quality.
> Efficient resource allocation: Prioritizing tests based on risk allows teams to allocate resources effectively, ensuring that testing efforts are focused where they are needed most.
> Enhanced collaboration: Collaborative risk management and testing ensure that all perspectives are considered, leading to more effective mitigation strategies.

Conclusion

Effective risk management in Agile development requires a focus on testing what is most important. By prioritizing tests based on risk, implementing automated and exploratory testing, and continuously monitoring and adjusting risk responses, Agile teams can proactively identify, assess, and mitigate risks. Understanding and implementing these strategies is key to achieving successful project outcomes and continuous improvement in Agile environments.

5.4. Delivering value to stakeholders

Delivering value to stakeholders is a fundamental goal of Agile development. Agile methodologies prioritize customer satisfaction, continuous delivery, and adaptability, ensuring that the software meets stakeholder needs and provides tangible benefits. This chapter explores strategies and best practices for delivering value to stakeholders in Agile environments.

Principles of value delivery in Agile

Agile value delivery is guided by several key principles:

➢ Customer collaboration: Agile emphasizes close collaboration with stakeholders to understand their needs and expectations. This ensures that the software aligns with business goals and delivers meaningful value.
➢ Iterative delivery: Agile teams deliver software incrementally, providing stakeholders with frequent updates and opportunities to provide feedback. This iterative approach allows for continuous improvement and adaptation.
➢ Prioritization: Agile prioritizes work based on business value, focusing on delivering the most important features first. This ensures that stakeholders receive the highest value early in the project.
➢ Transparency: Agile promotes transparency in communication and progress tracking, keeping

71

stakeholders informed and engaged throughout the development process.

5.4.1. Strategies for delivering value

Stakeholder engagement

➤ Regular communication: Maintain regular communication with stakeholders through meetings, demos, and updates. This ensures that stakeholders are informed and can provide feedback.
➤ Collaborative planning: Involve stakeholders in planning sessions, such as sprint planning and backlog grooming. This helps align the team's work with stakeholder priorities and expectations.

Value-driven prioritization

➤ Prioritize backlog items: Use techniques like MoSCoW (must have, should have, could have, won't have) to prioritize backlog items based on their value to stakeholders.
➤ Value stream mapping: Implement value stream mapping to visualize the flow of value through the development process. Identify and eliminate bottlenecks to optimize value delivery.

Iterative delivery and feedback

➤ Frequent releases: Deliver software in small, frequent increments to provide stakeholders with regular updates and opportunities to provide feedback.
➤ Sprint reviews: Conduct sprint reviews to demonstrate completed work and gather stakeholder feedback. Use this feedback to refine and improve the product.

Transparency and visibility

> Information radiators: Use information radiators, such as Kanban boards and burndown charts, to provide visibility into project progress and status.
> Clear reporting: Provide clear and concise reports on progress, risks, and changes. This keeps stakeholders informed and engaged.

Continuous improvement

> Retrospectives: Conduct regular retrospectives to reflect on the team's performance and identify areas for improvement. Implement changes based on feedback and lessons learned.
> Adaptability: Be flexible and adapt to changing stakeholder needs and priorities. This ensures that the software remains relevant and valuable.

Conclusion

Delivering value to stakeholders is a core principle of Agile development. By engaging stakeholders, prioritizing work based on value, delivering software iteratively, and maintaining transparency, Agile teams can ensure that their projects meet stakeholder needs and provide tangible benefits. Understanding and implementing these strategies is key to achieving successful project outcomes and continuous improvement in Agile environments.

6. Trends in software development management

The landscape of software development management is continuously evolving, driven by technological advancements, changing methodologies, and emerging industry needs. As we look towards the future, several key trends are poised to shape the way software development managers lead their teams and deliver value. This chapter explores some of the most significant trends expected to influence software development management in the coming years.

AI-powered development

Artificial Intelligence (AI) is revolutionizing software development by enhancing code quality, accelerating development cycles, and democratizing coding. Key aspects of AI-powered development include:

➢ AI-assisted coding: Tools like GitHub Copilot and Amazon CodeWhisperer provide intelligent code suggestions, reducing development time and improving code quality.
➢ Automated debugging: AI-powered debugging tools identify and fix bugs with greater precision, reducing human errors and increasing reliability.
➢ Natural language programming: Platforms like ChatGPT and Claude enable non-developers to create functional applications using natural language prompts, making coding more accessible.

DevOps evolves into platform engineering

DevOps practices are evolving to address the challenges of managing infrastructure and pipelines at scale. This evolution is giving rise to platform engineering, which focuses on providing a unified developer experience. Key elements include:

➢ Self-service tools: Dedicated platform teams provide self-service tools and standardized environments, streamlining workflows for developers.
➢ Infrastructure-as-Code (IaC): Advanced IaC frameworks incorporate AI and predictive analytics, enhancing scalability and resilience.

> Developer productivity: Automated CI/CD pipelines and platform engineering practices allow developers to spend more time on innovation and less on operations.

Integration of AI in project management

AI is not only transforming coding but also project management. AI-driven tools are optimizing project planning, resource allocation, and risk management. Key applications include:

> Predictive analytics: AI-powered project management tools use predictive analytics to optimize timelines, identify potential risks, and allocate resources effectively.
> AIOps solutions: AI-driven operations (AIOps) solutions detect anomalies and recommend system fixes, reducing downtime and increasing reliability.
> Enhanced decision-making: AI provides insights and recommendations that enhance decision-making, helping managers make data-driven choices.

Low-code and no-code Platforms

The rise of low-code and no-code platforms is democratizing software development, allowing non-developers to create applications without extensive programming knowledge. Key benefits include:

> Rapid prototyping: These platforms enable rapid prototyping, allowing teams to test concepts quickly and iterate based on feedback.
> Automating workflows: Businesses use low-code/no-code platforms to automate internal workflows and routine processes, improving efficiency.
> Market-ready solutions: Organizations can develop market-ready solutions without the need for full-scale engineering teams, reducing time-to-market

Cloud-native development

Cloud-native development is becoming the standard, with a significant shift towards building applications that leverage cloud infrastructure. Key trends include:

➢ Microservices architecture: Cloud-native applications are often built using microservices architecture, enabling greater scalability and flexibility.
➢ Serverless computing: Serverless architecture allows developers to focus on coding without managing servers, boosting scalability and efficiency.
➢ Increased cloud adoption: The adoption of cloud platforms continues to grow, driven by the need for quicker deployment and scalable applications.

Emphasis on security and compliance

As cyber threats become more sophisticated, there is an increasing emphasis on security and compliance in software development. Key trends include:

➢ DevSecOps: Integrating security practices into the DevOps pipeline (DevSecOps) ensures that security is considered at every stage of development.
➢ Automated security testing: Automated security testing tools identify vulnerabilities early in the development process, reducing the risk of security breaches.
➢ Regulatory compliance: Organizations are focusing on compliance with regulations such as GDPR, CCPA, and HIPAA to protect user data and avoid legal issues

Conclusion

The future of software development management is shaped by technological advancements, evolving methodologies, and changing industry needs. By embracing AI-powered development, platform engineering, hyper-agile practices, AI-driven project management, low-code/no-code platforms, cloud-native development, and enhanced security measures, software development managers can lead their teams to success in an increasingly complex and dynamic environment. Staying updated with these trends and continuously adapting to new challenges will be essential for delivering high-quality software that meets stakeholder needs and provides tangible value.

7. Final thoughts

Being a successful software development manager requires a combination of technical knowledge, leadership skills, and a commitment to continuous improvement. By embracing continuous learning, fostering collaboration, prioritizing people, focusing on delivering value, adapting and innovating, practicing effective risk management, and leading with empathy, you can guide your team to achieve remarkable results.

Remember, the journey of a software development manager is one of growth and learning. Stay curious, be open to new ideas, and always strive to be the best leader you can be. Your efforts will not only lead to successful projects but also create a positive and fulfilling work environment for your team.

8. About the author

The role of Software Development Manager is both fascinating and challenging. I have had the opportunity to lead software development in a small startup that grew from 5 to 120 employees, as well as in a large S&P 500 corporation, managing multiple teams and overseeing major releases. In smaller organizations, a software development manager works closely with the teams, while in larger ones, they often manage managers and interact with senior technical and leadership figures. Regardless of the organization size, the focus remains on four key aspects: people, process, tools, and delivery. I hope that after reading this book, you will become a better software development manager. Good luck!

www.ingramcontent.com/pod-product-compliance
Lightning Source LLC
LaVergne TN
LVHW072051060326
832903LV00054B/388